The *Spirit of St. Louis* picked up speed. . . .

Halfway down the runway, Lindbergh pulled back the stick to take off. The plane's wheels left the ground—then touched down again.

A second time, the plane started up, only to bounce back on the ground.

The third time, the *Spirit of St. Louis* took off for real. The plane climbed higher and higher. It cleared the wires at the end of the runway by just twenty feet—and kept going!

Lindbergh's heart was pounding. He was off! He was on his way to Paris!

THE $25,000 FLIGHT

The most exciting, most inspiring,
most unbelievable stories . . .
are the ones that really happened!

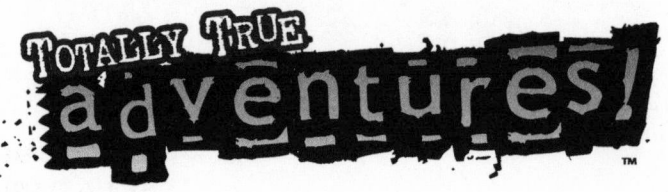

The $25,000 Flight
Babe Ruth and the Baseball Curse
Balto and the Great Race
The Curse of King Tut's Mummy
Finding the First T. Rex
The Titanic *Sinks!*

THE $25,000 FLIGHT

HOW LINDBERGH SET A DARING RECORD . . .

by Lori Haskins Houran • illustrated by Wesley Lowe

A STEPPING STONE BOOK™

Random House 🏠 New York

For the wise and wonderful Sarah Hopkins

Text copyright © 2014 by Lori Haskins Houran
Interior illustrations copyright © 2014 by Wesley Lowe

Photograph credits:
p. 78: some rights reserved by Jim, the Photographer; p. 80: some rights reserved by Matt Howey; p. 82: some rights reserved by Charles Atkeison μg; p. 85 (top): some rights reserved by dnak; p. 85 (bottom): some rights reserved by donjd2; pp. 90–94: courtesy of the Library of Congress, Prints & Photographs Division

Visit us on the Web!
SteppingStonesBooks.com
randomhouse.com/kids

Educators and librarians, for a variety of teaching tools,
visit us at RHTeachersLibrarians.com

Library of Congress Cataloging-in-Publication Data
Houran, Lori Haskins.
The $25,000 flight / Lori Haskins Houran.
p. cm. — (A stepping stone book)
ISBN 978-0-385-38284-7 (trade) — ISBN 978-0-385-38285-4 (lib. bdg.) —
ISBN 978-0-385-38286-1 (ebook)
1. Lindbergh, Charles A. (Charles Augustus), 1902–1974—Juvenile literature. 2. Air pilots—United States—Biography—Juvenile literature. 3. Transatlantic flights—History—20th century—Juvenile literature. 4. Aeronautics—Records—Juvenile literature.
I. Title. II. Title: Twenty-five thousand dollar flight.
TL540.L5H68 2014   629.1309163'1—dc23   2013029274

Printed in the United States of America
10 9 8 7 6 5 4 3 2 1

This book has been officially leveled by using the F&P Text Level Gradient™ Leveling System.

Contents

New York

Atlantic

Ocean

Paris

A Wish

Ten-year-old Charles Lindbergh stares up at the sky. An airplane is passing by. It's the first airplane he's ever seen.

Charles can't stop watching. His blue eyes shine. He feels a strange, strong pull in his chest. He wishes he was up there, soaring through the clouds!

Charles doesn't know it, but one day, he will get his wish.

One day, he will fly.

CHAPTER 1

The Prize

Charles Lindbergh had never set eyes on a plane until that day in 1912. He wasn't the only one. Few Americans had seen a plane up close. Hardly any had gone for a ride.

Airplanes were still a new invention. Orville Wright had flown the first plane in 1903. The flight lasted just twelve seconds.

Early airplanes were rickety. Their frail frames were made of wood and canvas. Their engines conked out with no warning. Crashes happened all the time.

Flying was much too dangerous for regular people. It was for risk takers, like the flying aces. The aces were daring pilots who fought in the skies in World War I.

Raymond Orteig admired these brave fliers. Orteig was not a pilot himself. He was a businessman—a very successful one.

Orteig moved to the United States from France when he was twelve years old. He took a job at a hotel, making a couple of dollars a week. He worked hard. By the time he was grown, he had enough money to buy hotels of his own.

One of these was the Hotel Lafayette in New York City. Pilots often gathered there. Orteig loved listening to the fliers tell stories. They talked about crashes they had survived. They talked about flights they planned to make. And they talked about prizes they wanted to win.

In those days, pilots won prizes for setting new records. Who would be the first pilot to fly half a mile? Two miles? Five miles?

As planes got better and better, the contests got bigger and bigger.

In 1909, London's *Daily Mail* newspaper gave a prize to the first pilot to cross the English Channel. It seemed like a long distance at the time—twenty-two miles.

In 1913, the *Daily Mail* set a new challenge. Fly across the Atlantic Ocean! Even at the shortest point, from Canada to Ireland, it was a whopping 1,900 miles.

It can't be done! some pilots said. *Yes, it can!* others insisted.

All the talk got Orteig thinking. He wanted

to come up with a prize of his own. It could connect the two countries he loved. France, where he was born. And America, where he had made his fortune.

On May 22, 1919, Orteig made his offer. He would give $25,000 to the first pilot to fly nonstop between New York and Paris, France!

Twenty-five thousand dollars was a lot of money. But the challenge was tough. It was nearly twice as long as the *Daily Mail* one. Pilots had to fly the 1,900 miles across the Atlantic. Plus 1,700 *more* miles. All without stopping!

Three weeks after Orteig's offer, a pair of pilots tried for the *Daily Mail* prize. They took off from Canada. On their way across the Atlantic, they got lost. They ran into storms. They faced freezing temperatures. At last, they crash-landed in a bog in Ireland. They had made it. But it was a horrible trip.

It showed just how hard Orteig's challenge was. Flying all the way from New York to Paris seemed impossible!

Years passed.

Planes got speedier and sturdier. Pilots gained more knowledge and skill. Some pilots began talking about the Orteig Prize. A few even said they were going to go for it. But none did.

Then, in 1926, a French flying ace named René Fonck stepped forward. He was ready to fly from New York to Paris!

Fonck was already known the world over. He had been a top fighter pilot in World War I. He shot down more enemy planes than any other pilot. His nickname was the Ace of Aces.

Newspapers raved about Fonck's fancy

plane, which was built just for the Paris trip.

It's the most expensive airplane ever made! It has three *engines! It's decorated in red satin and leather! There's even a bed inside!*

On September 21, 1926, a crowd gathered at an airfield on Long Island, New York. People were excited. In just minutes, Fonck

would take off for Paris! Would he make it there without stopping? Would he snag the Orteig Prize?

Fonck's crew moved back and forth. They loaded the plane with baggage, gear, and presents for people in France. They took a hot dinner to eat when they landed. And a basket of croissants to enjoy along the way!

By the time it was packed up and filled with fuel, the huge plane weighed nearly 28,000 pounds.

Fonck climbed aboard, along with his crew. The four men waved good-bye.

Fonck taxied the plane down the run-way. But instead of taking off, the plane kept rolling—straight into a ditch.

Then it burst into flames!

Two of the men were killed. Fonck and the other man crawled from the burning plane, shaken but alive.

¤ ¤ ¤

Fonck's accident was terrifying. But it didn't stop him from going after the Orteig Prize. He began making plans to build another plane.

This time, he had a rival.

Explorer Richard E. Byrd had shot to fame earlier in the year for leading the first-ever flight to the North Pole. Now Byrd wanted to guide a flight from New York to Paris. He put together a crew. He ordered a three-engine airplane of his own.

After years of no takers, now *two* famous fliers were trying for the Orteig Prize. And they weren't alone. In both America and France, pilots began rushing to prepare flights across the Atlantic.

The race was on!

CHAPTER 2

Stunts and Scrapes

Far from the excitement, in St. Louis, Missouri, Charles Lindbergh heard about the prize.

Four years before, in 1922, his boyhood wish had come true. He had taken a ride in an airplane. That one ride told Lindbergh what he had suspected all along: he belonged in the sky.

Lindbergh started flight school that spring. He soaked up everything he could about planes. How they worked. How to build and repair them. And, of course, how to fly them. By summer, he had a job as a barnstormer.

Barnstormers were pilots who flew from town to town. They sold rides and did stunts. For five dollars, they took people up in the air, swooping them above their friends and family.

Lindbergh and a friend barnstormed their way across Montana, Kansas, Colorado, and Wyoming. They tossed signs out the window of their plane. The signs read DAREDEVIL LINDBERGH in big letters.

Lindbergh lived up to his nickname. With his friend at the controls, he walked out onto a wing of the plane!

Then he stayed on the wing . . . while the plane flew a loop-de-loop!

These stunts looked dangerous. But Lindbergh insisted they weren't. Wing-walking was no harder than climbing a tree on a windy day, he said.

As for the loop-de-loops, Lindbergh made himself a special harness that attached to the plane. He slipped into the harness before the plane went upside down. He knew he was safe, even if the people on the ground didn't.

Lindbergh learned how to use a parachute. He thought skydiving would make a great trick for his act.

Soon he was leaping from the plane in midair! Crowds gasped and covered their eyes. Then Lindbergh popped open his parachute and fluttered to the ground.

Performing was fun, and Lindbergh was a terrific stunt flier. But stunt flying wasn't what Lindbergh really wanted to do. He wanted to be a serious pilot. And he wanted to fly the

very best planes. Who had them? The army.

In 1924, Lindbergh left the wild world of barnstorming behind. He headed back to flight school, this time with the army. He studied even harder than before. He finished first in his class . . . though he almost didn't finish at all.

Eight days before graduation, Lindbergh was on a training flight. His plane and another plane collided! Both pilots jumped to safety. It was the first time Lindbergh used a parachute to save his life, not as a stunt.

It was the first time—but not the last.

Three months later, Lindbergh was working as a test pilot. He was trying a new type of airplane. All at once, the plane spun out of control. Lindbergh bailed out. He became the first person in the United States to rescue himself twice with a parachute.

And that wasn't all. Lindbergh took a job with the airmail service. Flying the mail was dangerous. Forty pilots had started delivering the mail in 1918. By 1926, thirty-one of them were dead.

One night, fog wrapped Lindbergh's plane in darkness. Another night, a fierce storm blew in without warning. Lindbergh parachuted from not one but *two* more planes!

After four scrapes with death, many pilots would have given up. But not Lindbergh. Flying made him so happy, he said, that the risk was worth it.

He was about to take his biggest risk yet.

In the fall of 1926, Lindbergh was flying the mail as usual. But he couldn't stop thinking about something.

The Orteig Prize.

What if he went for it?

He wasn't famous like Fonck or Byrd. He was only twenty-four years old. And he had been a pilot for less than five years.

Yet he had learned a lot from barnstorming, army training, and airmail flying.

He kept turning the idea over in his mind. Could he really do it? Was it a crazy dream?

Not long ago, he told himself, *just flying an airplane seemed a dream. But that dream turned into reality.*

Lindbergh made up his mind. He was going to join Byrd and the others in the race for the Orteig Prize!

Only with one big difference. He wasn't going to carry along a crew. Or even a copilot.

Lindbergh was going to fly from New York to Paris . . . *alone.*

CHAPTER 3

The *Spirit of St. Louis*

At the start of 1927, four teams were gearing up to fly for the Orteig Prize.

Fonck was out of the running for now. His plane wouldn't be ready until at least the summer. But Byrd and his crew were getting close. They planned to take off in the spring, most likely in May.

So did two other teams of American fliers. One was led by Clarence Chamberlin, the other by Noel Davis.

Another team was getting ready, too—in France. Charles Nungesser and his copilot, François Coli, wanted to take off in Paris and land in New York. That was allowed under Orteig's rules. The flight just had to be nonstop between the two places. Either direction was fine.

All these men had their plans—and their *planes*—under way.

Nungesser's plane

Chamberlin's plane

Davis's plane

Meanwhile, Charles Lindbergh had a problem. He couldn't get an airplane.

The issue wasn't money. Lindbergh had raised $15,000. That was enough to build a small single-engine plane. It was exactly the kind of plane he wanted to fly.

In Lindbergh's mind, three-engine airplanes were too heavy for the trip. They might take off all right, but the bulky planes were hard to control in rough weather.

Nearly everyone disagreed with Lindbergh, including the airplane companies. It was too dangerous to fly over the ocean with just one engine, they said. What if the engine failed halfway across?

Lindbergh argued that three engines just meant three times the chance of engine failure. No one listened.

An even bigger issue was Lindbergh's plan to fly solo. *That,* people said, was just plain *nuts.* The trip would take at least a day and a half. Who would give him breaks so he could rest? And who would navigate?

Lindbergh answered that he would rather carry extra fuel than an extra person. After all, one man's weight equaled 300 miles' worth of gas! He'd do all the flying and navigating himself.

To Lindbergh, it made perfect sense. But the companies wouldn't budge. They didn't want their names connected with such a risky project.

One after another, four companies refused to build him a plane.

By February, time was running out. Lindbergh was behind the other pilots in the race.

So far behind, he wrote, "that they don't even consider me in the running. Most of them don't know I exist."

Lindbergh was nearly ready to give up. But he had to try once more.

He sent a telegram to a tiny company in San Diego, California, called Ryan Airlines. He explained that he needed an airplane. Ryan replied that they were interested in building him one.

Of course, other companies had been interested, too . . . before they knew Lindbergh's plans.

Lindbergh went to California to visit Ryan Airlines. He told them all about the Orteig Prize and his plan to try for it alone.

To his surprise, they didn't turn him away. Instead, they got excited. They'd build his plane. And they'd work seven days a week to get it done as fast as possible!

Lindbergh could hardly believe it. He still had a shot at the prize!

He decided to stay in California while his airplane was being built. That way, he could keep an eye on things.

Meanwhile, he dove into the rest of his plans. First, he had to figure out how to find his way across the Atlantic.

He'd never flown over a big body of water before. He'd never flown a very long way over land, either. Most of his flights were short hops—a few hundred miles at a stretch.

On these trips, he checked a map beforehand. Then he followed the roads and railroad tracks below him to stay on course.

What would he do when there was nothing below him but sea?

He thought about asking for help. There was a navy base nearby. Surely the sailors there could teach him a thing or two about ocean navigation. But what if word got out that he didn't know what he was doing?

Plenty of people already thought his plan was rash. Some even thought he should be stopped. The last thing he needed was to give those people more reason to doubt him. What if they convinced Ryan Airlines not to build his plane?

No, he wouldn't ask for help. He'd figure it out on his own.

At a map shop, he bought charts of the Atlantic Ocean. He pored over the charts for hours. Then he went to the public library.

He read every book he could find about navigation.

Lindbergh plotted a route across the ocean. He broke it into hundred-mile sections. Each section should take about one hour to fly. He'd mark off the sections on a chart as he went along. And he'd use a compass to keep him flying in the right direction.

It was a simple plan. But Lindbergh felt sure it would work.

Next he tackled another problem—fuel. He needed to carry as much as possible without overloading his plane.

His route was 3,610 miles long. But he wanted enough gas to fly 4,000 miles, just in case. That meant carrying 450 gallons, which weighed nearly 3,000 pounds!

There was only one way to carry that much fuel. He'd have to carry hardly anything else. Lindbergh needed to get rid of every extra ounce.

To save weight, he bought a wicker chair instead of a regular pilot's seat. He made his own lightweight flying boots. He even tore the extra pages out of his notebook and cut the edges off his charts and maps!

There would be no fancy meals or baskets of croissants for Lindbergh. He would take just enough food and water to get by. And he wouldn't pack anything for Paris. Not even a toothbrush or a change of clothes. It seemed like bad luck to think about things he'd need after the flight anyway.

Some decisions were harder to make. Should he take a radio? No, he decided. It might not work, and it was very heavy.

How about an inflatable raft? Yes, in case he went down in the ocean. Though he wouldn't bother with oars.

A parachute? Lindbergh thought it over. Parachutes had saved his life four times. But they weighed twenty precious pounds. In the end, he left the parachute behind.

Lindbergh's scrimping paid off. His plane weighed less than the gas it ran on!

On April 28, Lindbergh's trim silver airplane

was finished and ready to fly. *Spirit of St. Louis* was painted on both sides in bold black letters.

It was a fitting name. Lindbergh had come up with the idea for his flight in St. Louis. And the money for the plane came from local businessmen there. They had believed in him before anyone else did.

The *Spirit of St. Louis* looked marvelous. But how would it fly?

CHAPTER 4

The Flyin' Fool

Lindbergh climbed into his brand-new plane. The cockpit was tiny. It was only three feet wide and a bit over four feet high. At six feet three inches tall, Lindbergh barely fit inside!

He rolled the *Spirit of St. Louis* down the runway and took off. Right away, Lindbergh was pleased. The little plane was powerful. Speedy, too. It flew 128 miles per hour. Faster than he had dared to expect.

Lindbergh put the plane through test after

test. Every time, the *Spirit of St. Louis* flew beautifully.

On May 10, Lindbergh took off from San Diego. After a quick stop in St. Louis, he would fly on to New York.

It was a long trip just to get to the starting line. More than 2,500 miles! But Lindbergh didn't mind. At last, he was joining the race for the Orteig Prize!

¤ ¤ ¤

Meanwhile, the other racers weren't having much luck.

On April 16, Byrd's airplane, the *America*, went down during a test flight. Byrd broke his wrist. Two of his crew members were badly hurt. The plane was banged up, too. It looked as though it might take weeks to fix.

Then, on April 24, Chamberlin had a scare.

He took two children up in his plane, the *Columbia,* just for fun. During takeoff, the left wheel of the plane came loose! Chamberlin made an emergency landing, skidding to a stop on one wheel. No one was hurt. And the plane was only slightly damaged. Still, it wasn't a good sign.

The worst day by far was April 26. Davis and his copilot took off for their final test flight. They had barely left the ground when they crashed into a swamp. Both men died.

April turned to May. The bad-luck streak finally seemed to end. On the morning of May 8, Nungesser and Coli left Paris in their plane, the *White Bird.* They were the first team to take off successfully for the Orteig Prize!

Nungesser and Coli were excellent pilots. Lindbergh felt sure they would win the prize. He was so sure that he began thinking of a new plan for the *Spirit of St. Louis*.

Maybe he would fly his plane across the Pacific Ocean instead of the Atlantic. There wouldn't be a reward, but at least he'd set a new record. . . .

The following night brought shocking news: Nungesser and Coli were missing. Somewhere between Paris and New York, they had vanished!

A search began. Navy ships from the United States, Canada, and France swept the Atlantic, hoping to spot the *White Bird*.

On May 12, with the hunt still on, Lindbergh landed in New York. The second he touched down, reporters crowded around his plane.

"Hey, Charles!" they shouted. "Give us a picture! Say something, Lindy!"

Lindbergh was surprised. No one had paid

attention to him before. What was going on?

It seemed the papers were tired of running grim stories about failed test flights and missing pilots. They wanted a new story, and a new face to go with it.

Charles Lindbergh was just the ticket. He was young. He was handsome. And he was the only pilot brave—or brainless—enough to try for the Orteig Prize alone.

"The Kid Flyer," the headlines called him. "Lucky Lindy." "The Flyin' Fool."

That last nickname bugged Lindbergh. He knew his choice to fly solo seemed reckless. But it wasn't. He had thought everything through. He had planned carefully for months.

Of course, the newspapers didn't say anything about that. One reporter made it sound as if Lindbergh would just shove a toothbrush in his pocket and take off.

(The reporter had no idea that Lindbergh wasn't even taking a toothbrush!)

In story after story, the papers said there was no way Lindbergh would make it to Paris. Alone? In a single-engine plane? Without a radio or a parachute? It was "suicide," the papers said.

They even picked on the *Spirit of St. Louis* for being so small and simple. They called it "a gas tank with wings."

¤ ¤ ¤

Lindbergh and his plane were getting the most headlines. But they weren't the only story in town.

By now, Byrd's and Chamberlin's planes had been fixed. The *America*, the *Columbia*, and the *Spirit of St. Louis* all sat on the ground in New York, ready to fly for the prize.

The newspapers were in a tizzy. Who would take off first?

The problem was, *none* of them could take off. Not until the weather changed. It was stormy over the Atlantic, with no sign of clearing.

Day after day, the men waited.

Meanwhile, Nungesser and Coli were still missing. Hope was fading. It seemed that the quest for the Orteig Prize had claimed two more lives.

Now the total was six. Fonck's two crewmen. Davis and his copilot. Nungesser and Coli.

The stakes for the prize were higher than ever. No one knew that better than the men waiting—and waiting, and waiting—to take off.

Chapter 5

Next Stop, Paris

Thursday, May 19, was another soggy, foggy day. It looked as though no one would take off anytime soon. Not for days, the weatherman said. Maybe weeks.

Lindbergh felt restless. He decided to go to a Broadway show that night with some friends.

Before the show, they called the weatherman one more time. He told them surprising news. It looked as though the skies might clear by early the next day!

The break in the weather wouldn't last long. Lindbergh needed to take off in the morning. Otherwise who knew when he'd get another chance.

Forget the Broadway show! Lindbergh and his friends rushed back to the airfield. On the way, they stopped at a drugstore. One of Lindbergh's friends ran in and bought him a bag of sandwiches for the flight.

At the airfield, they began fueling up the *Spirit of St. Louis.*

Lindbergh looked around. He figured he'd see Byrd and Chamberlin getting their planes ready, too. But there was no sign of them. Had they missed the change in the weather report, the way he almost did?

Around midnight, Lindbergh went to his

hotel to get some rest. But he couldn't sleep. His mind was whirling!

At 2:30 in the morning, he got up and headed back to the airfield. Even though it was dark and rainy, a crowd of people had gathered to watch him take off.

Lindbergh looked over the *Spirit of St. Louis* one last time. He found a problem.

He had bought a special compass for the trip. But it was fixed above his head. It was nearly impossible for him to see there.

What should he do? If only he had a mirror to put in front of him, on his instrument panel. Then he could read the compass in its reflection. But he didn't have a mirror that fit.

A young woman stepped out of the crowd. She took a small round makeup mirror from her purse. Would that work?

Yes!

Now, how to attach the mirror? Another stranger came to the rescue. He pulled a sticky wad of gum from his mouth. It wasn't a fancy solution, but it did the trick!

More and more people joined the crowd. Byrd and Chamberlin came by to wish Lindbergh luck.

Reporters swarmed the airfield, too. One of them asked Lindbergh whether his little sack of sandwiches would be enough for the trip.

"If I get to Paris, I won't need any more," Lindbergh answered. "And if I don't get to Paris, I won't need any more, either."

By 7:40 a.m., everything was ready. The plane was fully fueled. Lindbergh's few supplies were on board.

It was time to go.

Lindbergh climbed into the *Spirit of St. Louis*. He buckled his safety belt. He pulled on his flying helmet. He fit his goggles over his eyes.

Then, with a nod to the folks on the ground, he steered down the muddy runway. The same runway where Fonck's plane had crashed eight months before.

A tangle of telephone wires hung at the end of the runway. The plane would have to clear them to take off.

Lindbergh felt a stab of panic.

How had he thought his tiny plane could lift so much fuel? How would it ever get off the ground, let alone make it past those wires?

Lindbergh shoved the worries aside.

The *Spirit of St. Louis* picked up speed. Halfway down the runway, Lindbergh pulled back the stick to take off. The plane's wheels left the ground—then touched down again.

A second time, the plane started up, only to bounce back on the ground.

The third time, the *Spirit of St. Louis* took off for real. The plane climbed higher and higher. It cleared the wires at the end of the runway by just twenty feet—and kept going!

Lindbergh's heart was pounding. He was off! He was on his way to Paris!

He busied himself with his controls. Then he glanced out the window. To his surprise, he saw another plane!

The plane was carrying newspaper photographers. The photographers stuck their cameras out the windows. They started snapping his picture! For goodness' sake. How far did they plan to follow him?

Luckily, the newspaper plane soon turned back.

Lindbergh took a deep breath. At last, he was alone. Just himself, his plane, and the sky.

Chapter 6

Solo

The *Spirit of St. Louis* buzzed north. Lindbergh peered out the open window of his cockpit. He watched the states glide by under his plane. New York, Connecticut, Rhode Island, Massachusetts.

He was headed for Newfoundland, Canada. Newfoundland was the last piece of land he would see before he started across the Atlantic Ocean.

Once he made it across, he hoped to spot

the green fields of Ireland. Then he would fly over England and straight on to France.

But that was a long way off. It would take about twelve hours just to get to Newfoundland!

Lindbergh checked the time. One o'clock in the afternoon. Should he eat one of his sandwiches? No, not yet. But a sip of water sounded good.

He reached for his canteen. His hand brushed against the map resting on his knees. It fluttered toward the open window!

Quickly, he snatched it back. Phew! Imagine if he had to turn back now, all because of a lost map!

Then Lindbergh noticed something up ahead. A cluster of angry black storm clouds was gathering in the sky.

Soon a strong wind pitched the *Spirit of*

St. Louis around. To Lindbergh, it felt as though the storm was a dog, picking up his plane in its teeth like a rabbit!

Rain pounded the plane. Lightning split the sky. Lindbergh held on tight, keeping the *Spirit of St. Louis* as steady as possible.

Half an hour later, the storm was over. Lindbergh and his airplane were still in one piece.

Lindbergh flew on. And on. The hours passed. One hour. Two hours. Three, four, five.

The flying was smooth as Lindbergh neared Newfoundland. No storms in sight. But he had a problem worse than bad weather. Much worse.

He was falling asleep!

He shook his head. He stamped his feet. He took off his safety belt and shifted around in his wicker seat. He flew with one hand, then the other. Anything to keep himself alert.

It was no surprise Lindbergh felt tired. He hadn't slept the night before. And now night had come again.

But he couldn't give in. He couldn't!

Then Lindbergh saw something out the window. A glittering white iceberg! And another, and another! They were floating in the dark waters of the Atlantic Ocean.

Lindbergh forgot about being tired. He was too excited. No one had ever flown solo across the Atlantic. And he was about to try!

¤ ¤ ¤

Night fell as Lindbergh started across the ocean. The *Spirit of St. Louis* didn't have any lights. Except for the moon and the stars above and a small flashlight he used to check his maps, Lindbergh was in the dark.

Then his plane plunged into a huge cloud. It was cold in the cloud. Freezing cold.

Lindbergh shone his flashlight out the window. Ice! Ice was forming on his wings! If the *Spirit of St. Louis* froze up, it would crash for

certain. He had to get out of that cloud *now*.

Lindbergh turned the plane around as fast as he dared. *Careful,* he told himself. *Don't lose control!*

All at once, he burst into open sky. He was all right!

But for how long? He could see more ice clouds ahead. Enormous ones. For the first time, Lindbergh wondered if he should turn back. Was it too dangerous to keep going?

On the other hand, flying back to Newfoundland wouldn't be any picnic. There were ice clouds in that direction now, too.

He pressed on toward Paris.

Lindbergh weaved in and out of the deadly clouds. He made it past them, only to face his next problem.

A wall of fog. Fog so thick that he couldn't see out his window.

He had to fly blind, relying on his compass to stay on course. Were there more ice clouds ahead? Storms? He had no clue. All he could see was the inside of his cockpit.

The worst part of the fog was that it

brought back his old enemy, sleep. With nothing to see out the window, Lindbergh grew drowsier than ever.

He tried to force his eyelids open with his fingers. His eyes kept closing. Again and again, he fell asleep. Then he jerked awake and found his plane veering off course!

Lindbergh knew he had to do whatever it took to stay alert. He thrust the plane's stick forward and backward to shake himself up. He hit himself in the face—hard. Nothing helped.

He was so tired that he started getting dizzy. He was going to pass out! Desperate, he stuck his head out the window.

The blast of cold air woke him up. When he opened his eyes, he understood how close he had come to death. Suddenly, he didn't feel sleepy anymore. He felt awake and alive.

Lindbergh had been flying solo for twenty-four hours. He had a thousand miles left to go. But he was more determined than ever.

Nothing was going to stop him. Not storms, not ice, not fog. And certainly not sleep.

Chapter 7

Where Is Lindbergh?

Alone over the Atlantic, Lindbergh had no idea what was happening in the world.

He didn't know that his takeoff had sparked something. Something big.

Around the globe, people were amazed and inspired by what he was trying to do.

America was completely gripped. Even Americans who hadn't cared much about the flight before could suddenly think of nothing else.

In offices and schools, at shops and restaurants, everyone asked the same thing: *Where is Lindbergh? Is he all right?*

All day Friday, radio stations ran reports. *He's flying above Massachusetts! He's reached Newfoundland!*

But once Lindbergh hit the open ocean, there was nothing to do but wait. It was as if the whole world was holding its breath.

Then, early Saturday morning, Americans received a message from a ship out at sea. It had spotted Lindbergh! He was only five hundred miles from Ireland!

Millions whooped and wept at the good news. He was so close now. *Go, Lindy, go!*

¤ ¤ ¤

Lindbergh carried on. Sometimes he soared 10,000 feet above the ocean. Sometimes he skimmed just ten feet over the waves.

He was flying low when he saw something splash in the water beneath him. He looked again. It was a porpoise!

Lindbergh felt joy rush over him. It was so good to see another living creature!

Soon he spotted a seagull. Another sign of life! Could it mean that he was getting close to land? He thought he had at least two hours to go before he reached Ireland. Was he even heading in the right direction?

Lindbergh had a terrible thought. What if his navigation plan hadn't worked? Or what if, while he was fighting sleep, he had drifted way off course?

Then, just ahead, he saw a small fleet of fishing boats. Help was at hand!

Lindbergh circled over the boats. At first, he didn't see anyone aboard. Then he spied a man's face, staring up at him.

Lindbergh leaned out his window. "WHICH WAY IS IRELAND?" he yelled.

The man didn't answer. Lindbergh circled again. Still the man just stared, without saying a word.

Lindbergh realized something. The man might never have seen a plane before. He was probably too stunned to speak!

It was no use wasting time and gas circling around. Lindbergh would just keep going and hope that he was headed the right way.

He didn't have to hope for long. Less than an hour later, he saw land. And not just any land. Ahead lay fields of bright green grass. It could only be one place. Ireland!

Lindbergh had made it across the Atlantic! Now all he had to do was cruise over Ireland and England, and he'd reach France. In less than six hours, he could land in Paris!

He looked down at the villages below. The villagers looked back and waved. Lindbergh grinned. It was wonderful to see people and houses again.

He felt himself beginning to relax. The hardest part was over! All at once, he was starving. He hadn't eaten anything since he took off! He fished a sandwich out of his bag and ate it. He took a long drink from his canteen.

As he flew closer and closer to Paris, Lindbergh started to think about what he would do once he landed. He hadn't let himself think about it before. He'd just wanted to survive the trip.

Would there be anyone to meet him at the airport? He wasn't sure. He'd have to find a place to spend the night. He hoped there was a hotel nearby. He needed some fresh clothes, too. Maybe the next day he'd go sightseeing in Paris. . . .

And then one of Paris's most famous sights appeared in front of him. The Eiffel Tower, glowing in the night sky!

Lindbergh circled the Eiffel Tower. He began searching for the airport.

There it was!

He switched on his flashlight to check the instrument panel one last time. Then he nudged his plane toward the ground.

The airfield was dark, and it was hard to see. After a few bumps, Lindbergh landed the *Spirit of St. Louis* gently on the ground. It had been thirty-three hours, thirty minutes, and thirty seconds since he left New York.

The trip was over. He had won the Orteig Prize! He had flown nonstop from New York to Paris. And he had done it by himself!

Lindbergh was excited, and a little sad. The flight had been tough, long, and lonely. But it had been really thrilling, too. Now the thrill was over.

Lindbergh turned the plane around to taxi toward the airport. He hoped he could keep the *Spirit of St. Louis* there for the night.

As he turned, the lights from the airport lit up the field. For the first time, he could see ahead of him. What he saw shocked him. There were people running across the field. Thousands and thousands of them. They were running right at his plane!

Quickly, Lindbergh cut the engine so his propeller wouldn't slice through the crowd.

"LINDBERGH!" the crowd cried.

He opened the cockpit door. Before he could step outside, he was yanked from the plane. The crowd lifted him above their heads. They bounced him along like a beach ball! He tried to get back down to the ground, but he couldn't. He was helpless!

Two French pilots came to the rescue. One pulled Lindbergh's helmet off. He stuck it on an American man nearby. The crowd, thinking the man was Lindbergh, began to mob him instead!

Then the other pilot tossed a coat over Lindbergh's head. He hustled Lindbergh off the field, dodging 150,000 fans.

As they hurried away, they could hear the crowd chanting in the background.

"LIND-BERGH! LIND-BERGH! LIND-BERGH!"

Overnight, Charles Lindbergh had become a hero.

CHAPTER 8

The Lone Eagle

In America, the news broke. *Lindy did it!*

Strangers jumped up and down and hugged each other. Cars and boats honked their horns. Fire trucks blasted their sirens. Factories blew their whistles, and churches rang their bells.

People couldn't wait to read about the flight. In New York City, a man was robbed . . . for his newspaper!

In Harlem, a new dance broke out. It was quickly named the Lindy Hop.

On Long Island, a couple topped that by naming their newborn son Charles Lindbergh Hurley. Before the year was over, hundreds more babies were named after the pilot.

America went wild for the young man who had done the impossible. A young man who was now hidden under a jacket, thousands of miles away!

¤ ¤ ¤

Lindbergh's rescuers sneaked him through Paris. They made their way to the American embassy.

Lindbergh took a bath and put on a pair of the ambassador's pajamas. But his day wasn't over.

A group of reporters had tracked Lindbergh down. The ambassador wanted to tell them to go away. He was sure Lindbergh was too tired to talk. But Lindbergh said it was all right.

He joked around with the reporters. They asked him to sit down. He told them he'd spent enough time sitting! Then they asked about his incredible feat, and he made it sound easy.

"I had four sandwiches when I left New York," he said. "I only ate one and a half during the whole trip. I don't suppose I had time to eat any more. You know, it surprised me how short a distance it is to Europe."

The reporters loved it. They couldn't wait to write about Lindbergh. Or the Lone Eagle, as they now called him. Somehow the Flyin' Fool didn't fit anymore.

After a few minutes, the ambassador pushed the reporters out. Lindbergh finally went to bed. It was 4:15 in the morning, Paris time. He had been awake for sixty-three hours!

¤ ¤ ¤

The next few days were a blur. Lindbergh was pulled from party to party and parade to parade. He met the president of France. He was showered with awards. On Thursday, he received the key to the city of Paris. Close to a million people came to watch.

Soon it was time to leave. The king of Belgium had invited him to visit! Before he left Paris, there was something he wanted to do.

On Friday morning, Lindbergh borrowed a French plane and took it up over the airport. Then he put on a surprise stunt show! He swooped and spun. He flew loop-de-loops, thrilling the people on the ground. The ambassador wrote later, "I have an idea this was the happiest morning of his stay in Paris."

The next day, Lindbergh took off for Belgium in the *Spirit of St. Louis*. On his way, he dropped a handwritten note from the plane. The note read:

Good-bye! Dear Paris.
Ten thousand thanks for your
kindness to me.
Charles A. Lindbergh

Lindbergh made a royal stop in Belgium. Then he went on to London. There, he met the king and queen of England. King George V asked him a surprising question.

"Tell me," the king said. "There is one thing I want to know. How did you pee?" Lindbergh explained that he had taken a container along for just that purpose.

Everywhere Lindbergh went, he was greeted by huge crowds. Europe couldn't get enough of him. Invitations rolled in from countries all over the world. Everyone wanted Charles Lindbergh.

But America wanted him, too! The president of the United States, Calvin Coolidge, sent a ship to carry Lindbergh and his plane home.

On June 11, Lindbergh arrived in Washington, D.C. The city was jammed with fans. He rode in a parade to the Washington Monument, where President Coolidge made a speech.

The president called Lindbergh fearless.

He praised the pilot's "splendid" journey.

"And now, my fellow citizens, this young man has returned," said the president. The crowd roared.

President Coolidge honored Lindbergh by pinning the Distinguished Flying Cross to his chest. He was the first person ever to receive the award.

Two days later, Lindbergh went to New York. The city had declared it Lindbergh Day! Four million people lined the streets for a ticker-tape parade. They tossed 2,000 *tons* of confetti into the air! It was the biggest parade in the city's history.

Lindbergh enjoyed a rare moment of quiet on June 16. At a special ceremony, Raymond Orteig presented him with the $25,000 Orteig Prize.

"I take the greatest pleasure in handing you this check," said Orteig.

The race from New York to Paris was over, and the prize officially won.

¤ ¤ ¤

For Charles Lindbergh, it was just the beginning. But what about the other people in the race?

Two weeks after Lindbergh's flight, Chamberlin and a copilot took off from New York, bound for Europe. As Chamberlin's plane crossed the Atlantic, it passed over the ship that was carrying Lindbergh home to America! Chamberlin landed in Germany. His trip set a record for long-distance flight.

On June 29, it was Byrd's turn. He and a three-man crew headed to France. They wound up crashing off the coast and paddling to shore on a rubber raft. Still, they had done it.

Then Fonck was ready to go. His new plane was finally finished in September. He announced that he would fly it from New York to Paris . . . and back!

But the U.S. Navy put a stop to his plans. Lindbergh, Chamberlin, and Byrd had been successful. But many other pilots had tried and failed to cross the Atlantic. The navy was spending too much time rescuing people. From then on, only seaplanes—not land planes, like Fonck's—could make the attempt.

Fonck was crushed. He never did fly a plane across the Atlantic Ocean.

As for Nungesser and Coli, they were never found. Neither was their plane, the *White Bird*.

In 1928, a statue was placed at the airport in Paris where Nungesser and Coli took off. It is the same airport where Lindbergh landed less than two weeks later. Carved on the statue in French is a message honoring all three pilots:

To those who tried, and to the one who succeeded.

CHAPTER 9

The Lindbergh Boom

Charles Lindbergh didn't know quite what to do after he won the Orteig Prize.

He had plenty of choices. Offers poured in. Every company in America wanted him behind their products. He was even offered a starring role in a movie!

Lindbergh didn't want to be a movie star. He wasn't sure he wanted to be famous at all. But he was. So now what?

Maybe he could use his fame for a purpose.

What did he care most about? Airplanes. Lindbergh was sure that planes could be just as important as trains and cars.

Most Americans didn't believe it. They didn't think flying was a real way to travel. They thought it was a fad. Lindbergh decided to change that thinking. He would fly to every state in the country and talk about planes!

Lindbergh took off in the *Spirit of St. Louis* on July 20, 1927. He flew more than 22,000 miles and made 147 speeches.

At every stop, people flocked to meet the man who had flown solo across the Atlantic. In three months, about 30 million people went to see Lindbergh and his plane. That was one-quarter of all Americans!

Lindbergh was already a huge star. As he crisscrossed America, his fame kept growing.

At least 200 songs were written about him.

Schools, streets, bridges, parks, lakes, and towns were named after him.

The U.S. Postal Service made a "Lindbergh airmail" stamp. It was the first stamp to honor a living person.

Meanwhile, companies churned out Charles Lindbergh items. Toys, hats, games, pens, razors, watches. And people rushed to buy them.

After his flight, Lindbergh's famous face appeared everywhere!

The nation had Lindbergh fever!

But was his fame helping air travel, the way he hoped it would?

It was. Americans were starting to fly.

The year before Lindbergh won the prize, there were only about 6,000 air passengers in the United States.

Two years *after* Lindbergh's flight, that number rose to 173,000. And kept rising! People called it the Lindbergh Boom.

In 1928, Lindbergh took off for another tour to talk about flying. This time, he went to Latin America. He flew the *Spirit of St. Louis* to sixteen countries.

When he landed back in the United States, Lindbergh decided it was time to retire his trusty plane.

He gave the *Spirit of St. Louis* to the Smithsonian Institution. Today it is on display at the National Air and Space Museum in Washington, D.C.

◘ ◘ ◘

Visitors come from all over the world to see Lindbergh's famous plane.

Lindbergh had convinced Americans to take to the skies. As air travel took off, he helped it grow. He trained pilots. He designed airports. And he flew and flew and flew, all over the world. Trinidad. China. Iceland. He went just about everywhere, finding safe routes for airlines to fly.

Meanwhile, he was already dreaming about the next phase of flight—space travel.

In 1929, Lindbergh met a scientist named Robert H. Goddard. Goddard was trying to build rockets. He believed that one day a rocket could power a spaceship to the moon.

The newspapers made fun of Goddard. They called his ideas absurd. They said he needed to go back to high school to learn science.

Hearing that your ideas were foolish and

impossible? Lindbergh knew something about that.

Lindbergh decided to help Goddard. For more than fifteen years, he raised money for the scientist's rocket experiments. He urged Goddard to keep going. Today, Goddard is called the father of space flight. His work led the way for America to land a spacecraft on the moon in 1969!

This small spacecraft took NASA's Apollo 11 *astronauts to the moon's orbit.*

On that spacecraft was astronaut Neil Armstrong, the first man to walk on the moon. His childhood hero? Charles Lindbergh. Armstrong was thrilled to meet Lindbergh, just days after returning from space.

Lindbergh sent Armstrong a letter after they met. He wrote, "I wonder if you felt on the moon's surface as I did after landing at Paris in 1927—that I would like to have had more chance to look around."

Lindbergh died in 1974. But his story kept on inspiring people.

One of them was businessman Peter Diamandis. In 1994, Diamandis read *The Spirit of St. Louis,* a book Lindbergh wrote about his flight to Paris. Diamandis got an idea.

He went to St. Louis and announced a new prize, modeled after the Orteig Prize. This one was called the X PRIZE. He would award it to the first team of people to build their own ship and fly it into space. The amount? Ten million dollars!

Twenty-six teams from seven countries competed for the prize. An American team won in 2004. The winning spacecraft was called *SpaceShipOne*. It hangs at the National Air and Space Museum. Next to it is the *Spirit of St. Louis.*

Lindbergh's airplane looks humble alongside the gleaming spaceship.

It's hard to believe that the simple silver plane carried Charles Lindbergh all the way from New York to Paris . . . and into history.

SpaceShipOne *and the* Spirit of St. Louis *can be seen together in Washington, D.C.*

The Mirror and the Chewing Gum

Some people doubt the chewing gum story. Did Lindbergh really stick a mirror to his instrument panel with gum?

It did happen. At least, it says so in Lindbergh's book *The Spirit of St. Louis.* But the book doesn't say when. Was it the morning of the flight? Or a few days earlier?

And did the gum hold the mirror all the way to Paris? Or was it replaced with something stronger (and less gross)?

We may never know.

Much of what we *do* know about Lindbergh's flight is thanks to Lindbergh himself. He wrote two books about his trip. *We* was published in 1927. *The Spirit of St. Louis* followed in 1953.

TURN THE PAGE FOR MORE AMAZING FACTS!

THE $25,000 FLIGHT

THE ROARING TWENTIES

Lindbergh came to fame during one of America's wildest decades. When the 1920s began, the country was still reeling from World War I and a terrible flu epidemic. After all that misery, people wanted to cut loose! They flocked to nightclubs to hear jazz music. They danced the Charleston and the Lindy Hop—sometimes in dance marathons that lasted for days. Many young women became flappers. They cut their hair short and wore makeup and sparkly dresses. Gloom was out, and glamour was in!

FEATS AND FADS

It's no wonder people in the 1920s thought flying was just a fad. The decade was packed with them. Besides dance marathons, there were rocking chair derbies, yo-yo competitions, even gum-chewing contests. One minute everyone was into mah-jongg, a Chinese tile game. The next minute, crossword puzzles were the rage. Possibly the strangest fad? Pole-sitting. Alvin "Shipwreck" Kelly started the trend in 1924, sitting on top of a flagpole for more than thirteen hours. Later, he set a much longer record—forty-nine days!

FAMOUS FACES

Charles Lindbergh was the biggest celebrity of the era. But there were plenty of other famous faces, among them baseball player Babe Ruth, jazz musician Louis Armstrong, silent-film

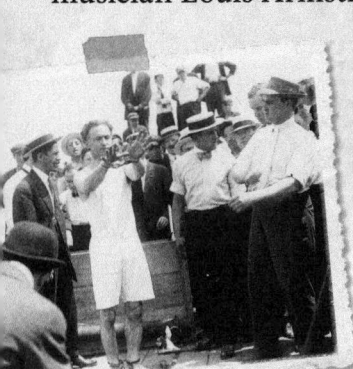

star Charlie Chaplin, and magician Harry Houdini. The most *infamous* face belonged to gangster Al Capone. Capone led a powerful Chicago crime ring until he finally went to prison in 1932.

WOMEN ON THE MOVE

Flappers showed the world that girls could have a good time. Other women had more serious goals in mind. Suffragettes fought for—and won—women's right to vote. Nineteen-year-old Gertrude Ederle became the first female to swim across the English Channel. And Amelia Earhart crossed the Atlantic Ocean by plane, earning the nickname Lady Lindy.

TAKING OFF

Lindy and Lady Lindy didn't know each other well, though they did meet. Lindbergh met most of the well-known pilots of the day. It's amazing to think that he knew Orville Wright, the first man to fly an airplane, and Neil Armstrong, the first man to walk on the moon. In Charles Lindbergh's lifetime, flight truly took off!

THE HISTORY OF FLIGHT: A TIMELIN

December 17, 1903
Orville Wright makes the
first airplane flight. It lasts
twelve seconds and covers
120 feet.

November 18, 1913
Lincoln Beachey flies
the first loop-de-loop.

July 25, 1909
Louis Blériot flies the
first plane across the
English Channel from
England to France.

May 5, 1961
Alan B. Shepard Jr. is the
first American to travel
into space.

October 11, 1958
NASA launches its first
spacecraft, *Pioneer I.*

April 12, 1961
Yuri Gagarin, in the *Vostok I*
spacecraft, is the first human
to orbit Earth.

October 4, 1957
Russia launches *Sputnik
the first man-made satel

February 20, 1962
John H. Glenn Jr. is
the first American to
orbit Earth.

December 21–27, 1968
Apollo 8 is the first manned
flight to orbit the moon.

July 20, 1969
Astronauts Neil Armstrong a
Buzz Aldrin, in *Apollo 11*, ar
the first humans to walk on t
moon. "That's one small step
man, one giant leap for manki

March 19, 1964
Geraldine F. Mock is the
first woman to fly around
the world in an airplane.

May 22, 1919
aymond Orteig offers a
25,000 prize to anyone
e to fly nonstop between
w York and Paris, France.

September 21, 1926
René Fonck tries for the
Orteig Prize, but fails.

May 20–21, 1927
Charles A. Lindbergh
flies the first nonstop solo
flight across the Atlantic.

May 2–3, 1923
Oakley Kelly and John Macready
make the first nonstop coast-to-coast
flight, from New York to San Diego,
in twenty-six hours, fifty minutes.

October 14, 1947
Charles E. Yeager is the
first to fly faster than the
eed of sound in a rocket-
powered plane.

May 20–21, 1932
Amelia Earhart is the
first woman to fly solo
across the Atlantic.

March 22, 1946
The first American-built rocket
leaves Earth's atmosphere,
reaching an altitude of fifty miles.

June 18–24, 1983
Sally K. Ride becomes
the first American
female astronaut.

April 17, 1970
he crew of the famous
Apollo 13 mission safely
returns to Earth.

October 4, 2004
SpaceShipOne is the first craft
to fly into space twice within two
weeks. It wins the ten-million-
dollar X PRIZE.

Acknowledgments

Thank you to Dorothy S. Cochrane of the National Air and Space Museum for her expert help with this book.

Many sources were useful in researching this story. The following books were especially helpful: Richard Bak's *The Big Jump: Lindbergh and the Great Atlantic Air Race*, A. Scott Berg's *Lindbergh*, Thomas Kessner's *The Flight of the Century: Charles Lindbergh and the Rise of American Aviation*, and of course, Charles A. Lindbergh's *The Spirit of St. Louis*.

About the Author

Lori Haskins Houran has never piloted a plane, though she did jump out of one once. (And only once.)

Lori has written more than twenty books for young readers, including *A Trip into Space* and *Dig Those Dinosaurs*. She lives in Florida with her two sons, who are not allowed to skydive until they are at least forty years old.

Get ready for more

Apollo 13

The astronauts heard a sharp *BANG!*

The spacecraft quaked and shuddered.

All over the control panel, warning lights were flashing like crazy. Dozens of alarms began beeping all at once. Jim Lovell looked over at Jack Swigert. Swigert's eyes were wide with fear.

Swigert spoke over radio to Mission Control in Houston. He had a hard time controlling the shakiness in his voice. "I believe we've had a problem here," he said.

"This is Houston. Say again, please," they asked.

Lovell answered. "Ah, Houston, we've had a problem. . . ."